Updated Philippines Travel Guide

Lucas Everhart

Updated Philippines Travel Guide

A Comprehensive Guide to Explore the Rich History, iconic tourist spots, Natural Wonders, Vibrant Culture, and Stunning Landscapes of Philippines and Travel Tips from Locals

By

Lucas Everhart

Disclaimer:

The information provided in this book, "Updated Philippines Travel Guide," is for general informational purposes only. While I have made every effort to ensure the accuracy and timeliness of the information, I do not make any representations or warranties of any kind, express or implied, about the completeness, accuracy, reliability, suitability, or availability of the information contained in this guide. Any reliance you place on such information is strictly at your own risk.

The book serves as a guide and should not substitute professional advice or serve as a guarantee of the conditions, safety, or quality of the destinations, accommodations, services, or activities mentioned. I disclaim any liability for any loss, injury, or inconvenience sustained by any reader as a result of the information or advice presented in this book.

It is recommended that readers independently verify and confirm any important information, such as visa requirements, health and safety guidelines, and local laws and regulations, before traveling to Philippines. The author shall not be held liable for any inaccuracies or changes in the information provided.

Table of Content

Introduction

The Philippines, located in Southeast Asia, is a captivating archipelago comprising more than 7,000 islands. Known for its stunning natural landscapes, warm hospitality, and rich cultural heritage, the Philippines offers a diverse array of experiences for travelers.

One of the country's most striking features is its breathtaking scenery. From pristine white sand beaches and turquoise waters to lush mountains and cascading waterfalls, the Philippines is a paradise for nature enthusiasts. Popular destinations such as Palawan, Boracay, and Siargao are renowned for their idyllic beaches and thriving marine life, making them ideal for swimming, snorkeling, and diving. The Chocolate Hills in Bohol and the rice terraces in Banaue are iconic landmarks that showcase the country's unique geological formations and agricultural heritage.

Beyond its natural beauty, the Philippines boasts a rich cultural tapestry shaped by its complex history. Influences from Spanish, American, and indigenous cultures have resulted in a vibrant blend of traditions, festivals, and cuisine. Visitors can immerse themselves in the colonial charm of Intramuros in Manila or explore the ancestral homes and cobblestone streets of Vigan. Festivals like the Ati-Atihan in Kalibo and Sinulog in Cebu showcase the country's exuberant spirit, featuring colorful parades, traditional dances, and vibrant costumes.

The warmth and friendliness of the Filipino people leave a lasting impression on visitors. Known for their hospitality, Filipinos go out of their way to make travelers feel welcome and at home. Engaging with locals offers an opportunity to gain insights into their way of life, traditions, and values.

The Philippines also offers a diverse range of activities for adventure seekers. From hiking the volcanic peaks of Mount Mayon or Mount Pinatubo to surfing the legendary waves of Cloud 9 in Siargao, there's something to suit every thrill-seeker's taste. The country's rich marine biodiversity provides opportunities for diving and snorkeling enthusiasts to explore vibrant coral reefs teeming with colorful marine life.

As with any travel destination, it's important to be mindful of local customs and travel responsibly. Taking steps to support sustainable tourism initiatives and respecting the environment and local communities ensures a positive and meaningful experience in the Philippines.

The Philippines is a captivating destination that offers a blend of natural beauty, cultural richness, and warm hospitality. Whether you seek relaxation on pristine beaches, adventure in the great outdoors, or cultural immersion in historical sites and traditions, the Philippines has something to offer every traveler.

Why You Should Visit The Philippines

There are countless reasons why you should consider visiting the Philippines, a captivating destination that offers a unique and unforgettable travel experience.

First and foremost, the Philippines boasts an abundance of natural beauty. From its stunning beaches with crystal-clear waters and powdery white sand to its lush mountains, cascading waterfalls, and breathtaking rice terraces, the country is a paradise for nature lovers. Whether you're seeking relaxation, adventure, or awe-inspiring landscapes, the Philippines has it all. Imagine lounging on the picture-perfect beaches of Boracay, exploring the underground river in Puerto Princesa, or swimming with whale sharks in Donsol—it's an opportunity to immerse yourself in some of the most extraordinary natural wonders on the planet.

Furthermore, the warmth and hospitality of the Filipino people make a visit to the Philippines truly special. Filipinos are known for their friendly and welcoming nature, and their genuine hospitality will leave a lasting impression on you. Interacting with locals offers a chance to learn about their rich culture, traditions, and way of life, creating meaningful connections and lifelong memories.

The Philippines is also a destination for food enthusiasts. Filipino cuisine is a delightful fusion of flavors, combining influences from Spanish, Chinese, and Southeast Asian culinary traditions. From mouthwatering dishes like adobo (marinated meat), sinigang (sour soup), and lechon (roast pig) to delectable street food and tropical fruits, the country offers a diverse and exciting culinary journey.

Moreover, the Philippines provides ample opportunities for adventure and outdoor activities. Whether it's hiking to the summit of Mount Pulag, exploring underground river systems, diving in world-class dive sites, or surfing epic waves, adrenaline junkies will find plenty of thrilling experiences to indulge in.

The Philippines offers a rich cultural tapestry and a fascinating history. Explore the colonial architecture of Intramuros in Manila, visit UNESCO World Heritage Sites such as the rice terraces of Banaue or the churches of Paoay, and witness colorful festivals showcasing traditional dances, music, and costumes.

The Philippines is a destination that offers a diverse range of attractions and experiences. From its natural wonders and warm hospitality to its vibrant culture and exciting adventures, the country is a treasure trove waiting to be discovered. So, pack your bags and get ready for an extraordinary journey through the stunning landscapes and vibrant culture of the Philippines.

How to Use This Guide

To make the most of this Philippines Travel Guide, here are some tips on how to effectively use it:

1. Familiarize Yourself

Begin by familiarizing yourself with the structure and layout of the guide. Take a look at the table of contents to get an overview of the topics covered and the chapters included.

2. Identify Your Interests

Determine what aspects of the Philippines you are most interested in exploring. Are you drawn to the beaches, cultural sites, adventure activities, or local cuisine? Knowing your preferences will help you navigate the guide more efficiently and focus on the sections that cater to your interests.

3. Plan Your Itinerary

Once you have identified your interests, use the guide to plan your itinerary. Start with the chapter that covers the region you intend to visit, such as Luzon, Visayas, or Mindanao. Within each chapter, you'll find information on specific destinations, attractions, and activities. Make notes and create a personalized travel plan based on the recommendations provided.

4. Seek Practical Information

In addition to providing insights into popular destinations, the guide offers practical information that will enhance your trip. Look out for chapters or sections dedicated to topics like transportation, accommodation, budgeting, safety tips, and local customs. These will help you navigate logistics and ensure a smooth and enjoyable travel experience.

5. Be Open to Discoveries

While the guide offers a comprehensive overview, be open to unexpected discoveries and serendipitous encounters. The Philippines is a dynamic and ever-evolving country, and new attractions, restaurants, or experiences may have emerged since the guide's publication. Embrace spontaneity and be willing to deviate from your initial plans to embrace the unexpected wonders of the Philippines.

Remember, this guide is a tool to enhance your travel experience, but the real adventure lies in your exploration and personal discoveries.

PLANNING YOUR TRIP

When planning your trip to the Philippines, careful preparation and research can go a long way in ensuring a smooth and unforgettable experience. This section will guide you through the essential steps of planning your journey. From understanding the country's diverse regions and climate to obtaining necessary travel documents and ensuring your health and safety, this chapter will provide you with valuable insights and practical tips. By taking the time to plan ahead, you'll be well-equipped to make the most of your time in this captivating archipelago and create cherished memories that will last a lifetime.

Understanding the Philippines

Understanding the Philippines goes beyond its stunning landscapes and warm hospitality. To truly appreciate this diverse archipelago, it's essential to delve into its history, culture, and society.

The Philippines has a rich and complex history influenced by various colonial powers. Spanish colonization, lasting over three centuries, has left a significant impact on the country's culture, religion, and language. The Spanish influence is particularly evident in the country's predominant religion, Roman Catholicism, and its colonial-era architecture seen in cities like Manila and Vigan.

The American period, following the Spanish-American War, introduced new political and educational systems, shaping the country's governance and educational institutions. English became widely spoken and remained one of the official languages alongside Filipino, a standardized version of Tagalog.

The Philippines is also known for its vibrant cultural traditions and festivals. Each region has its own distinct customs and celebrations, often showcasing a mix of indigenous, Spanish, and religious influences. Festivals such as Sinulog in Cebu, Ati-Atihan in Kalibo, and Panagbenga in

Baguio highlight the country's exuberance, featuring colorful parades, music, dance, and traditional costumes.

Filipino cuisine is a reflection of the country's cultural diversity. It combines indigenous ingredients and cooking techniques with influences from Spanish, Chinese, Malay, and American cuisines. Adobo, a savory dish marinated in vinegar and soy sauce, is considered the national dish, while other popular dishes include sinigang (sour soup), lechon (roast pig), and halo-halo (a refreshing dessert).

Understanding the social dynamics and cultural nuances of the Philippines is also important. The concept of "bayanihan," or communal unity and cooperation, is deeply rooted in Filipino society. Respect for elders and strong family ties are highly valued, as is the concept of "pakikisama" or harmonious relationships.

By delving into the history, culture, and social fabric of the Philippines, travelers can develop a deeper appreciation for its people and their way of life. This understanding enhances the overall travel experience, fostering meaningful connections and a greater sense of cultural immersion.

When to Visit

The Philippines is a year-round destination, but understanding the climate and weather patterns will help you determine the best time to visit based on your preferences and desired activities.

The country has two main seasons: the dry season and the wet season. The dry season, which is generally considered the peak tourist season, runs from November to April. During this time, the weather is typically warm and sunny, making it ideal for beach activities, island hopping, and exploring outdoor attractions. The months of December to February are particularly popular due to cooler temperatures and the festive holiday season.

The wet season, also known as the typhoon season, occurs from May to October. This period brings more rainfall and higher humidity, with the peak of typhoon activity usually between July and September. While the wet season can bring occasional downpours, it also offers lush landscapes, fewer crowds, and lower travel costs. If you're willing to embrace the occasional rain shower, the wet season can still be a great time to visit, especially for activities such as surfing, waterfall trekking, and enjoying the vibrant greenery.

It's important to note that the Philippines is an archipelago, and weather conditions can vary across different regions. Some areas, such as Batanes and the Cordillera region, have a different climate pattern, with milder temperatures and cooler weather throughout the year.

When planning your visit, consider your priorities. If you prefer sunny and dry weather, aim for the dry season. However, if you don't mind occasional rain and want to avoid crowds, the wet season can offer unique advantages. Be sure to check local weather forecasts and stay informed about any travel advisories or typhoon warnings.

Ultimately, the Philippines offers something special in every season, so choose the time that aligns with your preferences and embrace the unique experiences that each season brings.

Visa Requirements and Travel Documents

Before traveling to the Philippines, it's crucial to familiarize yourself with the visa requirements and necessary travel documents. Here's an overview to help you prepare for your trip:

1. Visa Exemption

Citizens of several countries, including the United States, Canada, Australia, and most European countries, are granted visa-free entry to the Philippines for a specific duration of stay. This typically ranges from 30 to 90 days, depending on the nationality. However, it's essential to check the latest visa regulations, as they can be subject to change.

2. Visa-on-Arrival

Some nationalities that are not eligible for visa-free entry can obtain a visa upon arrival at designated ports of entry. The visa-on-arrival allows for a stay of up to 30 days. However, it's advisable to confirm your eligibility and any specific requirements in advance.

3. Pre-Arranged Visa

For longer stays or specific purposes such as employment, study, or business, it may be necessary to obtain a pre-arranged visa from a Philippine embassy or consulate in your home country before your trip. Different types of visas are available depending on the purpose and duration of your stay. Check the website of the Philippine embassy or consulate in your country for detailed information and application procedures.

4. Passport Validity

Ensure that your passport is valid for at least six months beyond your planned departure date from the Philippines. This requirement is enforced by immigration authorities.

5. Return Ticket and Proof of Accommodation

Immigration officers may ask for proof of onward travel, such as a return ticket or an itinerary indicating your departure from the Philippines. It's also advisable to have proof of accommodation for the duration of your stay.

6. Other Requirements

Depending on your travel itinerary, you may need additional documents. For example, if you plan to engage in volunteer work or certain activities, you might need additional permits or clearances. Check with the Philippine embassy or consulate in your home country for specific requirements related to your travel plans.

It's essential to review the latest visa requirements well in advance of your trip and ensure that you have all the necessary documents to avoid any inconveniences or issues at immigration checkpoints.

Health and Safety

Considerations

When traveling to the Philippines, it's important to prioritize your health and safety. Here are some key considerations to keep in mind:

1. Vaccinations

Before traveling, consult with a healthcare professional to ensure that you are up to date on routine vaccinations. Additional vaccinations, such as hepatitis A and B, typhoid, and tetanus, may be recommended depending on the areas you plan to visit and the activities you'll engage in.

2. Travel Insurance

It's strongly advised to obtain comprehensive travel insurance that covers medical expenses, trip cancellation or interruption, and emergency evacuation. Ensure that the insurance policy provides adequate coverage for your specific needs and activities.

3. Medications and Health Kit

If you take prescription medications, bring an ample supply for the duration of your trip. It's also wise to carry a basic health kit with essential items like pain relievers, antihistamines, anti-diarrheal medication, and any personal medical supplies you may require.

4. Food and Water Safety

To prevent foodborne illnesses, practice good hygiene and be cautious about the food and beverages you consume. Stick to bottled or purified water, avoid eating raw or undercooked foods, and opt for hot, freshly prepared meals. Wash your hands regularly, especially before eating.

5. Mosquito-borne Diseases

The Philippines is home to mosquitoes that can transmit diseases such as dengue fever and malaria. Protect yourself by using insect repellent, wearing long-sleeved clothing and pants, and staying in accommodations with screened windows or air conditioning. Consider sleeping under a mosquito net, especially in rural or forested areas.

6. Travel Advisories and Safety Precautions

Stay informed about travel advisories and safety guidelines issued by your government and local authorities. Be aware of your surroundings, avoid high-risk areas, and take necessary precautions to protect your personal belongings. It's advisable to register with your embassy or consulate upon arrival.

By staying vigilant, following health and safety recommendations, and using common sense, you can ensure a safe and enjoyable trip to the Philippines.

Travel Insurance

When planning a trip to the Philippines, obtaining travel insurance is a crucial step to protect yourself and your investment. Travel insurance provides financial coverage and assistance in case of unexpected events or emergencies during your journey.

Comprehensive travel insurance for the Philippines typically includes coverage for medical expenses, trip cancellation or interruption, emergency medical evacuation, baggage loss or delay, and personal liability. It offers peace of mind by mitigating the financial burden that can arise from unforeseen circumstances such as accidents, illnesses, or travel disruptions.

In the Philippines, where adventure activities and outdoor exploration are popular, having travel insurance becomes even more important. Whether you're planning to hike mountains, dive in pristine waters, or engage in water sports, travel insurance can provide coverage for medical emergencies or evacuation in remote areas.

Before purchasing travel insurance, carefully review the policy to understand the coverage limits, exclusions, and any pre-existing conditions clauses. Consider factors such as the duration of your trip, the activities you plan to undertake, and the value of your belongings.

Ensure that your travel insurance policy adequately covers your needs and aligns with the activities and destinations you intend to visit in the Philippines. Travel insurance offers invaluable protection, giving you the confidence to explore and enjoy your trip, knowing that you have financial coverage and assistance in case of unforeseen events.

Essential Tips for Traveling in the Philippines

When traveling to the Philippines, keep these essential tips in mind to ensure a smooth and enjoyable experience:

1. Plan Ahead

Research your destinations, create a travel itinerary, and make necessary reservations in advance. The Philippines offers a wide range of attractions and activities, so planning ahead will help you make the most of your time.

2. Pack Accordingly

Pack lightweight and breathable clothing suitable for the tropical climate. Don't forget essentials like sunscreen, insect repellent, a hat, and comfortable footwear, especially if you plan on exploring nature or hiking. Remember to pack any necessary medications and travel documents.

3. Respect the Local Culture

The Philippines is a culturally diverse country with various customs and traditions. Respect local customs, dress modestly when visiting religious sites, and be mindful of cultural sensitivities. Learning a few basic Filipino phrases can also go a long way in building rapport with locals.

4. Stay Hydrated and Practice Food Safety

Drink plenty of bottled or purified water to stay hydrated in the tropical climate. Be cautious about street food and ensure that you consume food from clean and reputable establishments to avoid foodborne illnesses. Peel fruits or wash them thoroughly before eating.

5. Use Reliable Transportation

Public transportation options vary across different regions of the Philippines. Research and choose reliable transportation modes such as metered taxis, reputable ride-hailing services, or accredited transportation companies. For inter-island travel, domestic flights and ferries are common options.

6. Stay Aware of Your Surroundings

While the Philippines is generally a safe destination, it's important to stay aware of your surroundings, particularly in crowded or unfamiliar areas. Keep an eye on your belongings, use lockers or hotel safes to secure valuables, and be cautious when withdrawing money from ATMs.

7. Embrace Filipino Hospitality

Filipinos are known for their warm hospitality, so embrace the friendliness and kindness of the locals. Don't hesitate to ask for assistance or recommendations—they are often eager to help and share their insights.

By following these essential tips, you can make the most of your journey through the Philippines and create lasting memories of this beautiful and diverse country.

Getting to the Philippines

Getting to the Philippines is relatively easy, with several international airports serving as gateways to the country. Here are the common ways to reach the Philippines:

1. International Flights

The Ninoy Aquino International Airport (NAIA) in Manila is the primary international gateway, with numerous airlines offering direct flights from major cities worldwide. Other international airports, such as Mactan-Cebu International Airport, Clark International Airport, and Puerto Princesa International Airport, also have international connections.

2. Connecting Flights

If there are no direct flights from your location, you can consider connecting flights via major Asian hubs like Singapore, Hong Kong, Kuala Lumpur, or Seoul. Connecting flights provide convenient access to various destinations in the Philippines.

3. Cruise Ships

Some travelers opt to reach the Philippines via cruise ships. Popular ports of call include Manila, Boracay, Puerto Princesa, and Cebu. Cruise itineraries often include multiple destinations within the Philippines and other Southeast Asian countries.

4. Overland Travel

Overland travel to the Philippines is limited due to its island geography. However, it is possible to reach the country by land from neighboring countries such as Malaysia and Indonesia through ferry connections.

5. Domestic Flights

Once you arrive in the Philippines, domestic flights are available to reach different islands and destinations within the country. Airlines like Philippine Airlines, Cebu Pacific, and AirAsia Philippines operate domestic flights to major cities and tourist destinations.

It's important to check visa requirements and travel advisories for your specific nationality and origin before planning your trip to the Philippines. Additionally, consider booking your flights in advance to secure the best deals and make sure to arrive at the airport with sufficient time for check-in and immigration procedures.

By choosing the most convenient mode of transportation and planning your journey accordingly, you'll be well on your way to experiencing the beauty and wonders of the Philippines.

OVERVIEW OF MANILA

Manila, the capital city of the Philippines, is a bustling metropolis that blends a rich historical heritage with modern developments. From its Spanish colonial roots to its vibrant cultural scene and thriving commercial districts, Manila offers a diverse range of experiences. Explore the well-preserved historical sites of Intramuros, delve into the city's multicultural heritage in Chinatown, and indulge in the local culinary delights. With its impressive shopping malls, entertainment venues, and lively festivals, Manila serves as a gateway to the Philippines, offering visitors a captivating introduction to the country's vibrant culture and dynamic energy.

Historical Landmarks and Museums

Manila, the capital city of the Philippines, is home to numerous historical landmarks and museums that showcase the rich cultural heritage of the country. Here are some notable sites to explore:

1. Intramuros

The walled city of Intramuros is a must-visit historical landmark. Built during the Spanish colonial era, it features well-preserved architecture, cobblestone streets, and significant sites like Fort Santiago, a former military fortress, and San Agustin Church, a UNESCO World Heritage site known for its beautiful Baroque architecture.

2. Rizal Park

Located in the heart of Manila, Rizal Park is a national park dedicated to the country's national hero, Dr. Jose Rizal. The park features a monument honoring Rizal, lush gardens, fountains, and statues. It is a popular spot for relaxation, picnics, and cultural events.

3. National Museum of the Philippines

The National Museum is the country's premier museum complex. It houses an extensive collection of art, archaeological artifacts, and historical exhibits that showcase the Philippines' cultural heritage. Highlights include the Spoliarium by Juan Luna, an iconic masterpiece, and the anthropology and natural history exhibits.

4. Ayala Museum

Situated in Makati City, the Ayala Museum offers an immersive experience in Philippine art, culture, and history. It features interactive exhibits, dioramas, and galleries that cover various periods, including pre-colonial times, the Spanish colonial era, and the contemporary art scene.

5. Casa Manila

Located within the Intramuros district, Casa Manila is a reconstructed Spanish colonial house that provides a glimpse into the lifestyle of the Filipino elite during the Spanish period. It showcases period furniture, decorative arts, and architectural details that recreate the ambiance of the era.

6. Bahay Tsinoy

This museum highlights the Chinese-Filipino heritage and its contribution to Philippine history. It houses exhibits on Chinese-Filipino culture, art, and history, including artifacts, photographs, and multimedia presentations.

These historical landmarks and museums in Manila offer a fascinating journey through the Philippines' past, providing insights into its diverse cultural influences and significant historical events. Exploring these sites is an enriching experience that deepens one's understanding of the country's heritage.

Vibrant Neighborhoods and Markets

Manila, the capital city of the Philippines, is a vibrant metropolis with diverse neighborhoods and bustling markets that offer a glimpse into the local culture and lifestyle. Here are some of the vibrant neighborhoods and markets to explore in Manila:

1. Binondo

Known as the world's oldest Chinatown, Binondo is a vibrant neighborhood brimming with Chinese-Filipino culture and history. Explore its narrow streets filled with traditional Chinese shops, restaurants, and temples. Binondo is famous for its authentic Chinese cuisine and bustling food scene, making it a haven for food enthusiasts.

2. Makati

As the financial and commercial center of Manila, Makati is a dynamic neighborhood with towering skyscrapers, upscale shopping malls, and trendy restaurants. Explore the bustling streets of Ayala Avenue and Bonifacio Global City (BGC), where you'll find a mix of international and local brands, art galleries, and a vibrant nightlife scene.

3. Intramuros

Step back in time by visiting Intramuros, the historic walled city of Manila. This neighborhood features well-preserved

Spanish colonial architecture, cobblestone streets, and significant landmarks like Fort Santiago and San Agustin Church. Explore the charming streets on foot or take a guided horse-drawn carriage tour (kalesa) to experience the area's historic charm.

4. Divisoria

Known as a bustling bargain hunter's paradise, Divisoria is a sprawling market district where you can find a wide variety of goods at affordable prices. From clothing, accessories, and home décor to fresh produce and street food, Divisoria offers a vibrant and lively shopping experience.

5. Quiapo

Quiapo is a neighborhood famous for its vibrant street markets, most notably the Quiapo Market and the Quiapo Church. The market is known for its wide range of merchandise, including religious items, textiles, handicrafts, and local street food. Visit the Quiapo Church, home to the revered Black Nazarene statue, and witness the fervent devotion of Filipino Catholics.

Exploring these vibrant neighborhoods and markets in Manila provides a fascinating glimpse into the city's cultural diversity, culinary delights, and lively street life. Immerse yourself in the vibrant atmosphere and discover the unique charm of each neighborhood, offering a truly authentic Manila experience.

Shopping and Dining

Options

Manila, the capital city of the Philippines, offers a wide array of shopping and dining options that cater to every taste and budget. Whether you're looking for luxury brands, local crafts, or mouthwatering cuisine, Manila has something for everyone. Here are some highlights:

1. Shopping Malls

Manila is known for its numerous shopping malls, offering a one-stop shopping experience. SM Mall of Asia, one of the largest malls in Southeast Asia, features a vast selection of international and local brands, entertainment facilities, and a picturesque waterfront view. Other popular malls include Greenbelt, Glorietta, and Power Plant Mall, which offer a mix of high-end and mid-range retail stores, restaurants, and entertainment options.

2. Night Markets

For a unique shopping experience, head to Manila's night markets. Divisoria Night Market and Baclaran Market are bustling areas where you can find a wide range of goods at affordable prices, including clothing, accessories, toys, and home décor. These markets are particularly vibrant during the holiday season.

3. Artisanal Crafts

For locally made crafts and souvenirs, visit markets like the Salcedo Saturday Market and Legazpi Sunday Market. These markets showcase a variety of artisanal products, including handcrafted items, organic food products, and unique artworks.

4. Culinary Delights

Manila is a paradise for food lovers, offering a diverse culinary scene. From street food to fine dining, the city caters to all tastes. Explore food markets like Mercato Centrale and weekend markets like Banchetto to sample a wide range of local and international cuisine. Makati and Bonifacio Global City (BGC) are known for their upscale dining establishments, featuring cuisines from around the world.

5. Specialty Districts

Manila is also home to specialized shopping districts. For electronics and gadgets, visit Gilmore Avenue in Quezon City. For antiques and vintage finds, head to the shops along Evangelista Street in Makati. For affordable fashion, visit the trendy boutiques in the neighborhood of Cubao Expo.

In Manila, shopping and dining are not just activities but vibrant experiences that showcase the city's diversity and culinary prowess. Explore the various shopping destinations and indulge in the flavors of Manila, making your visit a memorable one.

Nightlife and Entertainment

Manila, the capital city of the Philippines, offers a vibrant and dynamic nightlife scene, with a plethora of entertainment options to suit various tastes. From energetic clubs and live music venues to lively bars and cultural performances, here's a glimpse into the nightlife and entertainment in Manila:

1. Poblacion, Makati

Poblacion is a thriving neighborhood known for its bustling nightlife. It is home to numerous bars, pubs, and speakeasies that cater to diverse preferences. Whether you're looking for craft cocktails, live music, or a lively atmosphere, Poblacion has it all.

2. Bonifacio Global City (BGC)

BGC is a vibrant district that comes alive at night. It features upscale bars, rooftop lounges, and trendy nightclubs. The Fort Strip and High Street are popular destinations for those seeking a dynamic nightlife experience.

3. Resorts World Manila

Located near the Ninoy Aquino International Airport, Resorts World Manila offers a wide range of entertainment options. The complex includes a casino, theaters showcasing local and international performances, live music venues, and a variety of restaurants and bars.

4. Cultural Performances

Experience the rich cultural heritage of the Philippines through traditional performances. The Cultural Center of the Philippines in Manila showcases dance, music, and theater performances that highlight Filipino artistry and talent.

5. Comedy Clubs

If you're in the mood for laughter, Manila has comedy clubs that feature local and international comedians. Enjoy a night of humor and entertainment at venues like Zirkoh Comedy Bar and The Comedy Manila.

6. Live Music

Manila has a vibrant live music scene with venues offering various genres. Check out popular spots like 70s Bistro, Route 196, and Saguijo for a dose of live performances from local bands and artists.

It's important to note that nightlife options may vary depending on the current circumstances and regulations. Always check for updated information and follow local guidelines to ensure a safe and enjoyable experience.

Manila's nightlife and entertainment scene provides an exciting blend of music, performances, and vibrant venues, ensuring a memorable experience for locals and visitors alike.

LUZON: THE NORTHERN

PHILIPPINES

Luzon, the largest and most populous island in the Philippines, is a region of diverse landscapes, cultural heritage, and exciting attractions. Located in the northern part of the country, Luzon offers a multitude of experiences for travelers. From the bustling capital city of Manila to the stunning natural wonders such as the Banaue Rice Terraces and Mount Pinatubo, Luzon is a destination that encompasses both modernity and natural beauty. With its rich history, vibrant cities, scenic landscapes, and warm hospitality, Luzon is a captivating region that showcases the charm and diversity of the Northern Philippines.

Exploring the Cordillera Region

The Cordillera Region in the northern part of Luzon, Philippines, is a captivating destination offering a unique blend of natural beauty, rich cultural heritage, and adventurous activities. With its stunning mountain landscapes, cascading waterfalls, and picturesque rice terraces, the Cordillera Region is a paradise for nature enthusiasts and avid trekkers.

One of the highlights of exploring this region is the chance to witness the magnificent Banaue Rice Terraces, a UNESCO World Heritage site. These ancient terraces, carved into the mountainside by the indigenous Ifugao people, are a testament to their remarkable engineering skills and sustainable farming practices.

The Cordillera Region is also home to charming towns like Sagada, known for its hanging coffins and breathtaking caves, and Baguio City, the "Summer Capital of the Philippines," offering cool temperatures, stunning gardens, and a vibrant arts scene.

Immerse yourself in the rich cultural heritage of the region by visiting indigenous communities, such as the Ifugao and Kalinga tribes, where you can learn about their traditional customs, vibrant festivals, and intricate craftsmanship.

Adventure seekers can embark on challenging hikes to conquer the peaks of Mount Pulag or explore the mystical beauty of the Sumaguing Cave in Sagada.

Exploring the Cordillera Region promises a blend of natural wonders, cultural immersion, and thrilling adventures, making it a must-visit destination for those seeking a unique and enriching travel experience in the Philippines.

Banaue and the Rice Terraces

Banaue, located in the Cordillera mountain range of the Philippines, is a picturesque town renowned for its awe-inspiring rice terraces. These terraces, often referred to as the Banaue Rice Terraces, are an iconic UNESCO World Heritage site and a testament to the ancient agricultural practices of the indigenous Ifugao people.

The Banaue Rice Terraces is an engineering marvel that dates back over 2,000 years. Carved into the mountainsides by hand, these terraces are a stunning testament to the ingenuity and skill of the Ifugao people. They showcase the sustainable farming techniques employed by the community to cultivate rice on steep slopes.

Visiting Banaue offers a unique opportunity to immerse yourself in the rich cultural heritage of the Ifugao people. Interact with the locals and gain insights into their traditional farming practices, rituals, and way of life. You can also explore the quaint villages surrounding Banaue, such as Batad and Bangaan, where you'll find even more intricate rice terraces and traditional Ifugao houses.

Trekking through the lush green terraces provides a breathtaking experience, allowing you to witness the sheer grandeur of these man-made wonders. The viewpoints offer panoramic vistas, especially during sunrise and sunset, when the terraces are bathed in golden hues.

In addition to the rice terraces, Banaue town itself offers a charming ambiance. You can explore the town's market, where you'll find local handicrafts, souvenirs, and traditional woven products.

Banaue and its Rice Terraces are a captivating destination that showcases the beauty of nature and the rich cultural heritage of the Ifugao people. A visit to this remarkable site is a journey back in time and an opportunity to appreciate the remarkable achievements of ancient civilizations in harmonizing with their environment.

Sagada and its Caves

Sagada, a quaint town nestled in the mountains of the Cordillera Region in the Philippines, is a destination that entices travelers with its serene beauty and intriguing cave systems. Known for its stunning limestone formations, Sagada offers a unique experience for adventurers and nature lovers alike.

Sagada's cave systems are a major draw for visitors. The most famous among them is Sumaguing Cave, often referred to as the "Big Cave." Exploring Sumaguing Cave is an exhilarating experience as you navigate through underground rivers, climb rock formations, and witness mesmerizing stalactites and stalagmites. Marvel at the Cathedral, a massive chamber resembling a cathedral hall, and the Crystal Cave adorned with glistening mineral formations.

Aside from Sumaguing Cave, Sagada offers other notable caves to explore, such as Lumiang Cave and Crystal Cave. Lumiang Cave is known for its unique feature called the "Cave Connection," which involves traversing underground passages that link Lumiang Cave to Sumaguing Cave.

Sagada's caves also hold cultural significance. They serve as burial grounds for the local people, and the hanging coffins within the caves are a striking sight. These coffins, suspended on cliffs or placed in crevices, represent the ancient burial practices and traditions of the indigenous communities.

Beyond its cave systems, Sagada enchants visitors with its picturesque landscapes. Hiking trails lead to scenic viewpoints, waterfalls, and rice terraces. Echo Valley and Hanging Coffins offer a serene setting to appreciate nature and gain insights into the local customs.

Sagada's caves are a testament to the region's geological wonders and cultural heritage. Exploring these captivating underground realms provides an unforgettable adventure and a deeper appreciation for the natural beauty and cultural significance of Sagada in the Philippines.

Vigan's Colonial Charm

Vigan, located in the province of Ilocos Sur in the Philippines, is a city steeped in colonial charm and rich history. With its well-preserved Spanish-era architecture and cobblestone streets, Vigan offers a glimpse into the country's colonial past.

Vigan's most iconic feature is Calle Crisologo, a narrow street lined with centuries-old ancestral houses. Taking a stroll along this cobblestone street feels like stepping back in time. The houses, with their unique architectural styles and intricate details, reflect the city's Spanish colonial influence. Many of these houses have been converted into museums, shops, and guesthouses, allowing visitors to immerse themselves in the city's heritage.

Vigan's historic center, known as the Vigan Heritage Village, has been recognized as a UNESCO World Heritage site. The area is filled with well-preserved colonial structures, including St. Paul's Metropolitan Cathedral and the Archbishop's Palace. The plaza, Plaza Salcedo, is a central gathering place and often hosts cultural events and festivities.

Another must-visit attraction in Vigan is the Syquia Mansion Museum. This ancestral home provides a glimpse into the opulent lifestyle of the Filipino political dynasty, showcasing elegant furniture, artifacts, and memorabilia from the Syquia family.

To further explore Vigan's history, a visit to the Crisologo Museum is highly recommended. This museum exhibits the life and achievements of the Crisologo family, prominent figures in Philippine politics.

The city is also known for its culinary delights, with traditional dishes like empanada (a savory pastry filled with meat and vegetables) and Vigan longganisa (a local sausage) being popular choices among visitors.

Vigan's colonial charm and architectural beauty transport visitors to a bygone era. The city's commitment to preserving its heritage has made it a cultural gem and a favorite destination for those seeking a glimpse of the Philippines' colonial past.

Laoag and the Sand Dunes

Laoag, located in the province of Ilocos Norte in the Philippines, is a captivating destination known for its unique combination of historical attractions and natural wonders. One of its standout features is the impressive sand dunes that stretch along its coastline.

The La Paz Sand Dunes, situated just outside the city, offers a thrilling adventure in a landscape reminiscent of a desert. These expansive sand dunes, with their undulating peaks and valleys, provide an exciting playground for various activities. Visitors can embark on a thrilling 4x4 off-road adventure, speeding through the sandy terrain while experiencing heart-pounding drops and exhilarating turns. Sandboarding is also a popular activity, allowing you to glide down the dunes on a board for an adrenaline-pumping ride.

Aside from the sand dunes, Laoag boasts a rich history and cultural heritage. The St. William's Cathedral, with its distinct Sinking Bell Tower, stands as a symbol of the city's strong Catholic influence. The nearby Marcos Museum and Mausoleum honor the legacy of the late Philippine President Ferdinand Marcos.

Laoag's historic district features Spanish-era structures, including the iconic Tobacco Monopoly Monument and the

Juan Luna Shrine, which pays homage to the renowned Filipino painter.

For a taste of the local cuisine, try the famous Ilocos empanada, a savory pastry filled with a mixture of vegetables, meat, and egg. The bustling public market in Laoag is an ideal place to sample regional delicacies and purchase traditional handicrafts.

Laoag and its sand dunes offer a unique blend of adventure and cultural exploration. Whether you're seeking thrilling outdoor activities or a glimpse into the region's history, Laoag promises a memorable experience in the Philippines.

Beaches and Islands in Luzon

Luzon, the largest island in the Philippines, is not only known for its vibrant cities and stunning landscapes but also for its captivating beaches and picturesque islands. Here's a closer look at some of the top beach destinations in Luzon:

1. Pagudpud

Located in Ilocos Norte, Pagudpud is home to the renowned Saud Beach, often hailed as the "Boracay of the North." This pristine white sand beach boasts crystal-clear waters and stunning sunsets, making it a favorite among beach enthusiasts.

2. Zambales

Along the western coast of Luzon lies Zambales, offering a stretch of beautiful sandy beaches. Popular spots include Subic Bay, known for its water sports activities, and Anawangin Cove, famous for its scenic camping sites and unique landscape of pine trees against the white sand beach.

3. Batangas

Known as the "Diving Capital of the Philippines," Batangas is blessed with an array of stunning beaches and diving spots. Popular destinations include Anilao, where divers can explore vibrant coral reefs, and Nasugbu, known for its picturesque coves and luxurious beach resorts.

4. Pangasinan

Located in the western part of Luzon, Pangasinan is home to the Hundred Islands National Park. This archipelago offers breathtaking islands and pristine beaches perfect for island-hopping, swimming, snorkeling, and camping.

5. Baler

Situated on the east coast of Luzon, Baler is a haven for surfers. With its consistent waves, Sabang Beach attracts surf enthusiasts from around the world. The laid-back vibe and scenic surroundings make it an ideal beach getaway.

These are just a few of the many stunning beaches and islands waiting to be explored in Luzon. Whether you're seeking relaxation on powdery white sands or adventure in the waters, Luzon offers a diverse range of beach destinations to suit every traveler's preferences.

VISAYAS: THE

CENTRAL ISLANDS

Visayas, a cluster of islands located in the central part of the Philippines, is a region that offers a myriad of natural wonders, cultural treasures, and breathtaking beaches. Comprising several provinces and islands, including Cebu, Bohol, and Negros, Visayas is a popular destination for both domestic and international travelers. From pristine white sand beaches and vibrant coral reefs to historic landmarks and colorful festivals, Visayas showcases the rich diversity and beauty of the Philippines. Whether you're seeking adventure, relaxation, or cultural immersion, Visayas has something to offer for every type of traveler.

Cebu City and its Surroundings

Cebu City, the capital of the province of Cebu in the Visayas region of the Philippines, is a bustling metropolis that seamlessly blends modernity with a rich historical and cultural heritage.

Cebu City is known for its iconic historical sites, such as the Magellan's Cross, which marks the arrival of Christianity in the Philippines, and the Basilica Minore del Santo Niño, home to the oldest Catholic relic in the country. The Fort San Pedro, a Spanish colonial-era fortress, offers a glimpse into the city's past.

A visit to the Taoist Temple perched on a hillside, provides a serene escape with its colorful architecture and panoramic views of the city. The temple is an important center for the local Chinese community.

Cebu City is a shopper's paradise, with bustling markets like Carbon Market and upscale malls offering a wide range of products and souvenirs. Don't miss the chance to sample the famous Cebu lechon (roast pig), known for its crispy skin and succulent meat.

Just a short distance from Cebu City, you'll find Mactan Island, known for its beautiful beaches and world-class resorts. Take a dip in the turquoise waters, indulge in water sports activities, or simply relax under the sun.

For nature enthusiasts, a visit to the stunning Kawasan Falls in Badian is a must. This multi-tiered waterfall offers a refreshing retreat amidst lush greenery and turquoise pools.

Cebu City also serves as a gateway to other attractions in the region, such as the captivating island of Bohol, known for its Chocolate Hills and tarsier sanctuaries.

Cebu City and its surroundings offer a blend of history, culture, natural beauty, and modern amenities. With its vibrant cityscape and nearby attractions, Cebu City is a destination that caters to a variety of interests and promises an unforgettable experience in the Philippines.

Bohol's Natural Wonders

Bohol, an island province in the Central Visayas region of the Philippines, is renowned for its breathtaking natural wonders and unique attractions.

One of Bohol's most famous landmarks is the Chocolate Hills, a geological formation of over 1,000 perfectly conical hills that turn chocolate brown during the dry season. These iconic hills offer a surreal and picturesque landscape, best appreciated from the viewing deck in Carmen.

Bohol is also home to adorable and endangered Philippine tarsiers. Visit the Tarsier Conservation Area in Corella or the Philippine Tarsier and Wildlife Sanctuary in Loboc to observe these tiny primates in their natural habitat.

For those seeking tranquility, a cruise along the Loboc River is a must-do. Enjoy a relaxing boat ride while admiring the lush greenery, passing through charming villages, and savoring a buffet lunch or dinner on board.

Panglao Island, connected to Bohol by a bridge, is a popular beach destination. Its white sand beaches, crystal-clear waters, and vibrant coral reefs make it a paradise for snorkeling, diving, and sunbathing. Alona Beach is the most famous, offering a lively atmosphere and various water sports activities.

The Hinagdanan Cave, a naturally-formed underground cave with an enchanting pool of fresh water, provides an otherworldly experience. Explore the cave's stalactite and stalagmite formations while basking in the ethereal lighting.

Bohol also boasts stunning waterfalls, such as the enchanting Mag-Aso Falls in Antequera and the picturesque Camugao Falls in Balilihan. These cascades offer refreshing swimming spots and beautiful natural surroundings.

Bohol's natural wonders showcase the diversity and beauty of the Philippine archipelago. From the iconic Chocolate Hills to the adorable tarsiers, serene rivers, pristine beaches, and captivating caves and waterfalls, Bohol is a destination that promises an unforgettable experience for nature lovers and adventure seekers.

Dumaguete and Siquijor

Dumaguete and Siquijor are two enchanting destinations in the Philippines, known for their laid-back atmosphere, natural beauty, and rich cultural heritage.

Dumaguete, the capital of Negros Oriental, is often referred to as the "City of Gentle People." The city exudes a relaxed and friendly vibe, making it a popular destination for travelers seeking a peaceful getaway. Stroll along Rizal Boulevard, lined with restaurants and cafes, and enjoy the view of the ocean and the stunning sunsets. Explore the bustling Dumaguete Public Market, where you can find fresh produce, local delicacies, and handicrafts.

Dumaguete is also the gateway to several natural attractions. Just a short boat ride away lies Apo Island, a renowned marine sanctuary teeming with vibrant coral reefs and a variety of marine life. Snorkeling or diving in its waters is a must for nature enthusiasts.

Siquijor, an island province known as the "Mystic Island," offers a unique blend of natural beauty and folklore. With its pristine beaches, crystal-clear waters, and lush tropical landscapes, Siquijor is a paradise for beach lovers and nature enthusiasts. Explore Salagdoong Beach, known for its turquoise waters and cliff diving spots, or venture to Cambugahay Falls, where you can swim in its cascading turquoise pools.

Siquijor is also famous for its mystical traditions and healing rituals. Visit the century-old Balete Tree, believed to be enchanted, and have a fish spa experience by dipping your feet into the natural pool beneath it. Discover traditional folk healing practices and mystical traditions at the Siquijor Healing Festival.

Dumaguete and Siquijor offer a blend of natural beauty, cultural heritage, and tranquility. Whether you're seeking relaxation on beautiful beaches, exploring underwater wonders, or immersing yourself in local traditions, these destinations in the Philippines provide a memorable and enchanting experience.

Boracay's White Beach

Boracay's White Beach, located on the island of Boracay in the Philippines, is a world-renowned beach destination that has captivated travelers with its pristine beauty and idyllic tropical paradise.

Stretching for approximately four kilometers along the island's western coast, White Beach is famous for its powdery white sand and crystal-clear turquoise waters. The beach is divided into three stations: Station 1, Station 2, and Station 3, each with its own unique atmosphere.

Station 1 is known for its upscale resorts and quieter ambiance. The powdery white sand in this area is at its finest, making it perfect for sunbathing and strolling along the shore. Station 2 is the center of activity, bustling with restaurants, bars, and shops. Here, you can find a lively atmosphere and indulge in various water sports activities, such as parasailing, jet skiing, and paddleboarding. Station 3 offers a more laid-back vibe, with budget-friendly accommodations and a serene atmosphere.

White Beach is not just about sunbathing and swimming. The beachfront is lined with restaurants and bars that offer a wide range of dining options, from local Filipino cuisine to international dishes. As the sun sets, the beach comes alive with vibrant nightlife, with beach parties, fire dancers, and live music performances.

For those seeking adventure, there are numerous water sports activities available, such as snorkeling, scuba diving, and sailing. The nearby Bulabog Beach is a haven for kiteboarding and windsurfing enthusiasts.

Boracay's White Beach is a tropical paradise that offers a perfect combination of natural beauty, a vibrant atmosphere, and water sports activities. Whether you're seeking relaxation, adventure, or lively nightlife, White Beach is a must-visit destination in the Philippines that will leave you with unforgettable memories.

Exploring the Islands of Palawan

Palawan, known as the "Last Frontier" of the Philippines, is a province composed of stunning islands and natural wonders that have captured the imagination of travelers from around the world. Here's a glimpse into exploring the islands of Palawan:

1. El Nido

Located on the northern tip of Palawan, El Nido is renowned for its limestone cliffs, turquoise lagoons, and hidden beaches. Island-hopping tours take you to mesmerizing destinations like the Big Lagoon, Small Lagoon, Secret Lagoon, and Seven Commandos Beach, where you can snorkel, swim, and soak in the breathtaking scenery.

2. Coron

Situated in the Calamian Islands, Coron is famous for its crystal-clear waters and World War II shipwrecks. Snorkel or dive among these submerged relics and explore stunning sites like Barracuda Lake, Kayangan Lake, and Twin Lagoons. Coron is also home to beautiful beaches and the scenic Mount Tapyas viewpoint.

3. Puerto Princesa

The capital city of Palawan, Puerto Princesa, is known for its underground river, one of the New Seven Wonders of Nature. Take a boat tour through the Puerto Princesa Subterranean River National Park and marvel at the stunning limestone formations and diverse ecosystem.

4. Port Barton

A laid-back coastal village, Port Barton offers a tranquil beach getaway. Relax on the secluded beaches, go snorkeling or diving to explore the vibrant marine life, or take a boat trip to nearby islands and waterfalls.

5. Balabac

For those seeking off-the-beaten-path adventures, Balabac is a remote island group in southern Palawan. It boasts pristine beaches, turquoise waters, and an abundance of wildlife, including the endemic Philippine Mouse-Deer.

Palawan's islands showcase the natural beauty and biodiversity of the Philippines. With its stunning landscapes, crystal-clear waters, and diverse marine life, exploring the islands of Palawan is an unforgettable experience that will leave you in awe of the country's natural wonders.

MINDANAO: THE

SOUTHERN

PHILIPPINES

Mindanao, located in the southern part of the Philippines, is a region rich in cultural diversity, natural beauty, and captivating landscapes. Known as the "Land of Promise," Mindanao offers a unique travel experience for those seeking adventure, exploration, and immersion in the vibrant. traditions of the Philippines.

From the bustling city of Davao to the majestic Mount Apo, the highest peak in the country, Mindanao showcases a blend of stunning beaches, lush mountains, and fascinating cultural heritage. With its warm hospitality and off-the-beaten-path destinations, Mindanao invites travelers to discover a different side of the Philippines and create unforgettable memories.

Davao City and its Attractions

Davao City, located in Mindanao, the southern region of the Philippines, is a vibrant metropolis known for its natural beauty, rich culture, and diverse attractions. Here's a closer look at what makes Davao City a must-visit destination:

1. Mount Apo

Standing at over 2,954 meters, Mount Apo is the highest peak in the Philippines. Adventure seekers can embark on a challenging trek to the summit, rewarded with breathtaking views and an unforgettable sense of accomplishment.

2. People's Park

This urban green oasis offers a serene escape from the bustling city. The park features beautifully landscaped gardens, sculptures, and replicas of indigenous tribal houses, showcasing the cultural heritage of Mindanao.

3. Crocodile Park

Home to a vast collection of crocodiles, the Crocodile Park allows visitors to get up close and personal with these magnificent creatures. The park also houses other exotic animals, such as tigers, snakes, and birds.

4. Eden Nature Park

Nestled in the foothills of Mount Apo, Eden Nature Park is a paradise for nature lovers. Explore the lush gardens, enjoy outdoor activities like hiking and ziplining, and indulge in delicious organic meals sourced from the park's own vegetable and herb gardens.

5. Philippine Eagle Center

Located just outside the city, this conservation center is dedicated to protecting the endangered Philippine Eagle. Get an up-close look at these majestic birds and learn about ongoing conservation efforts.

6. Davao Chinatown

Immerse yourself in the vibrant Chinese-Filipino culture at Davao Chinatown. Sample delicious Chinese cuisine, browse through markets selling traditional goods, and witness colorful festivals and celebrations.

Davao City's blend of natural wonders, cultural attractions, and warm hospitality make it a captivating destination in the Philippines. Whether you're seeking adventure, cultural immersion, or a taste of local cuisine, Davao City has something for everyone.

Mount Apo and Other Natural Treasures

Mount Apo, standing at an impressive height of 2,954 meters, is not only the highest peak in the Philippines but also a natural treasure that beckons adventure enthusiasts from around the world. Located in Mindanao, the southern region of the Philippines, Mount Apo is part of a protected national park and offers a range of outdoor activities and breathtaking sights.

The climb to the summit of Mount Apo is a challenging yet rewarding experience. Trekkers will be treated to stunning panoramic views of lush forests, diverse flora and fauna, and a sense of accomplishment upon reaching the peak. The journey is filled with cascading waterfalls, pristine lakes, and unique rock formations, providing picturesque spots for rest and rejuvenation.

Aside from Mount Apo, Mindanao boasts other natural treasures that are worth exploring. The Enchanted River in Hinatuan is a mesmerizing blue river surrounded by lush vegetation, offering a tranquil atmosphere and a chance to witness vibrant marine life. The Aliwagwag Falls in Cateel is another natural wonder, known as the "Curtain Falls" due to its multi-tiered cascades that resemble a giant curtain.

For beach lovers, the white sand beaches of Siargao Island offer world-class surfing opportunities and a laid-back island atmosphere. Camiguin Island, known as the "Island Born of Fire," is dotted with volcanoes, hot springs, and pristine dive sites, making it a haven for nature and adventure enthusiasts.

Mindanao's natural treasures provide endless opportunities for exploration, adventure, and relaxation. From conquering the majestic Mount Apo to diving in vibrant marine ecosystems and unwinding on pristine beaches, this region of the Philippines is a paradise for nature lovers and outdoor enthusiasts.

Siargao's Surfing

Paradise

Siargao Island, located in the province of Surigao del Norte in the Philippines, is renowned as a surfing paradise and an idyllic tropical getaway.

Siargao is best known for its famous surf break, Cloud 9. This world-class wave attracts surfers from all corners of the globe, offering challenging barrels and thrilling rides. Cloud 9 has gained international recognition as one of the top surfing spots in the world, hosting annual surfing competitions that showcase the skill and talent of surfers.

Beyond Cloud 9, Siargao offers a variety of surf spots suitable for beginners and experienced surfers alike. Beaches like General Luna and Pacifico Beach provide consistent waves, making them ideal for learning and practicing your surfing skills. The island's warm tropical waters and pristine sandy beaches create a perfect backdrop for a memorable surfing experience.

Siargao's laid-back and rustic charm adds to its appeal. The island exudes a relaxed and bohemian vibe, with coconut palm-fringed beaches, vibrant sunsets, and a slow-paced lifestyle. Surfing communities have flourished, creating a vibrant surf culture where travelers can connect with like-minded individuals and share their love for the sport.

Aside from surfing, Siargao offers a range of activities to explore its natural beauty. Discover the enchanting Magpupungko Rock Pools, where you can swim in natural rock formations filled with crystal-clear waters. Take a boat tour to the stunning Sohoton Cove, home to enchanting lagoons, caves, and a thriving marine ecosystem.

Siargao's combination of world-class surf breaks, stunning natural landscapes, and a welcoming atmosphere make it a true surfing paradise in the Philippines. Whether you're a seasoned surfer or a beginner looking to catch your first wave, Siargao promises an unforgettable experience for surf enthusiasts and beach lovers alike.

Zamboanga City and its Cultural Heritage

Zamboanga City, located in the westernmost region of Mindanao in the Philippines, is a city rich in cultural heritage and known for its vibrant mix of cultures.

Zamboanga City is often referred to as "Asia's Latin City" due to its Spanish and Latin American influences. Spanish colonial architecture can be seen in its historic buildings, such as Fort Pilar, a well-preserved 17th-century fortress that serves as a shrine and museum showcasing the city's history. The city's signature landmark, the pink-hued Santa Cruz Island Lighthouse, is another architectural gem that adds to Zamboanga's charm.

The city's cultural diversity is evident in its colorful festivals and traditional practices. The Hermosa Festival, held in October, celebrates the city's patroness, Our Lady of the Pillar, with vibrant parades, street dancing, and cultural showcases. Visitors can immerse themselves in the rich cultural heritage of Zamboanga through traditional dances like the vinta dance, performed on colorful traditional boats known as vintas.

The Yakan Weaving Village provides a glimpse into the indigenous Yakan tribe's intricate art of weaving. Visitors can witness the creation of traditional Yakan textiles and even purchase unique handmade products as souvenirs.

Zamboanga City is also known for its delicious cuisine, influenced by Spanish, Malay, and Chinese flavors. Local delicacies like curacha (a type of crab) and satti (skewered meat served with a spicy sauce) offer a culinary adventure that reflects the city's cultural fusion.

Exploring Zamboanga City allows visitors to experience a blend of history, culture, and gastronomy. Its cultural heritage, warm hospitality, and diverse traditions make it a captivating destination for those seeking an authentic and immersive travel experience in the Philippines.

Adventure in Camiguin and Bukidnon

Camiguin and Bukidnon, two provinces in the Philippines, offer thrilling adventures and breathtaking landscapes for outdoor enthusiasts and nature lovers.

Camiguin, often referred to as the "Island Born of Fire," is known for its volcanic landscapes and natural wonders. Start your adventure by trekking up Mount Hibok-Hibok, an active volcano that offers a challenging hike and stunning panoramic views from the summit. Visit the Sunken Cemetery, where a coral-covered cemetery lies beneath the sea, creating a unique snorkeling and diving spot.

The island is also home to refreshing waterfalls, such as Katibawasan Falls and Tuasan Falls, where you can take a dip in cool, cascading waters. For an extraordinary experience, take a boat tour to the Mantigue Island Marine Sanctuary, where you can snorkel or dive among vibrant coral reefs and encounter diverse marine life.

Bukidnon, located in the highlands of Mindanao, offers a different kind of adventure. Embark on an exhilarating white-water rafting experience along the Cagayan de Oro River, navigating through rapids and enjoying the stunning scenery along the way. For nature lovers, explore the magnificent landscapes of Dahilayan Adventure Park, which offers zip-lining, tree-top walks, and ATV rides through lush forests.

Bukidnon is also known for its panoramic mountain views and the towering Mount Kitanglad, an ideal destination for trekking and bird watching. The province is home to various indigenous tribes, and visitors can immerse themselves in their culture and traditions by visiting tribal villages and participating in cultural exchanges.

Camiguin and Bukidnon provide a perfect blend of adventure and natural beauty. Whether you're seeking adrenaline-pumping activities, serene natural landscapes, or cultural encounters, these destinations offer a unique and memorable experience in the heart of the Philippines.

OFF THE BEATEN

PATH

While the Philippines is known for its popular tourist destinations, there are also hidden gems waiting to be discovered off the beaten path. These lesser-known locations offer a chance to escape the crowds and experience a more authentic side of the country. From secluded islands with pristine beaches to remote mountain villages with unique cultural traditions, exploring off the beaten path in the Philippines unveils a world of untouched beauty and enriching experiences. Whether you're an adventure seeker, nature lover, or cultural enthusiast, venturing off the beaten path in the Philippines opens doors to hidden treasures and unforgettable adventures.

Lesser-known Destinations in the Philippines

The Philippines is renowned for its popular tourist destinations like Boracay, Palawan, and Cebu. However, beyond these well-known spots, the country hides lesser-known destinations that are equally captivating. Here are some of the lesser-known gems in the Philippines:

1. Batanes

Situated in the northernmost part of the country, Batanes is a group of picturesque islands known for its rolling hills, breathtaking cliffs, and traditional stone houses. This remote destination offers a serene and untouched natural beauty, perfect for those seeking tranquility and stunning landscapes.

2. Siquijor

Often referred to as the "Mystic Island," Siquijor boasts pristine beaches, mystical waterfalls, and a rich cultural heritage. Explore enchanting caves, witness mesmerizing firefly displays, and learn about traditional healing practices believed to be practiced on the island.

3. Siargao's Sohoton Cove

While Siargao is well-known for its surfing spots, Sohoton Cove offers a hidden paradise. This enchanting cove is filled with mangrove forests, lagoons, and mysterious caves. Embark on a boat tour to witness bioluminescent plankton, swim in secluded lagoons, and marvel at unique rock formations.

4. Camiguin

Dubbed the "Island Born of Fire," Camiguin is a small island with a diverse range of natural attractions. Discover volcanoes, hot springs, waterfalls, and the sunken cemetery. Snorkel or dive in marine sanctuaries, and indulge in the island's sweet lanzones fruit, which is celebrated during the Lanzones Festival.

5. Dumaguete

Located in Negros Oriental, Dumaguete is a charming coastal city known for its laid-back atmosphere and university town vibes. Explore marine sanctuaries like Apo Island, visit stunning waterfalls like Casaroro Falls, and experience the vibrant arts and culture scene.

These lesser-known destinations in the Philippines offer unique experiences, pristine beauty, and a chance to escape the crowds. Venture beyond the popular tourist spots, and you'll be rewarded with hidden treasures and unforgettable adventures.

Remote Islands and
Hidden Beaches

The Philippines is home to a myriad of remote islands and hidden beaches that offer a slice of paradise for those seeking tranquility and seclusion. These untouched gems are perfect for nature lovers, beach enthusiasts, and adventurers looking to escape the crowds and discover pristine beauty. Here are some of the remote islands and hidden beaches in the Philippines worth exploring:

1. Calaguas Islands

Located off the coast of Camarines Norte, the Calaguas Islands boast powdery white sand beaches, crystal-clear turquoise waters, and a peaceful atmosphere. With limited infrastructure and fewer tourists, it's a perfect destination for beach camping and island hopping.

2. Palaui Island

Situated off the northeastern coast of Luzon, Palaui Island offers rugged landscapes, stunning cliffs, and secluded beaches. The island is a protected marine sanctuary, providing opportunities for snorkeling, diving, and wildlife spotting.

3. Dinagat Islands

Tucked away in the Caraga Region, the Dinagat Islands offer unspoiled beauty and a laid-back ambiance. Explore hidden coves, secret lagoons, and pristine beaches such as Bitaog Beach and Puyo Beach.

4. Balabac Islands

Located in Palawan, the Balabac Islands are a remote paradise featuring turquoise waters, coral reefs, and white sand beaches. Visit Onuk Island, Candaraman Island, or Punta Sebaring to experience untouched beauty and encounter diverse marine life.

5. Sibuyan Island

Known as the "Galapagos of Asia," Sibuyan Island in Romblon province is a haven for nature enthusiasts. Its lush forests, towering mountains, and hidden waterfalls provide a stunning backdrop for beach-hopping and eco-tourism activities.

These remote islands and hidden beaches offer a chance to disconnect from the bustling world and immerse oneself in the serenity of nature. Whether you're seeking solitude, adventure, or simply a stunning backdrop for relaxation, these hidden gems in the Philippines promise unforgettable experiences and a glimpse into the country's untouched beauty.

INDIGENOUS

COMMUNITIES AND

CULTURAL

EXPERIENCES

The Philippines is a diverse country with a rich cultural heritage, and one of the most fascinating aspects is its indigenous communities. These communities, with their unique traditions, beliefs, and way of life, offer a glimpse into the country's cultural tapestry. For travelers seeking authentic cultural experiences, here are some indigenous communities in the Philippines worth exploring:

Cordillera Region

The Cordillera region in northern Luzon is home to various indigenous tribes, including the Igorot people. Visit the Banaue Rice Terraces, a UNESCO World Heritage Site, and interact with the Ifugao people, known for their rice terrace farming techniques and intricate weaving.

1. Mindoro

The island of Mindoro is home to the Mangyan tribes, which comprise several groups such as the Iraya, Alangan, and Tadyawan. Experience their unique customs, traditional music, and handicrafts, and learn about their connection to nature.

2. Palawan

The indigenous communities in Palawan, such as the Tagbanua and Batak tribes, have a deep spiritual connection to the natural environment. Explore their villages, partake in cultural activities, and gain insights into their traditional knowledge of the land and sea.

3. Kalinga

Journey to Kalinga in the Cordillera region to encounter the Kalinga tribe. Known for their intricate body tattoos and vibrant cultural festivals, the Kalinga people offer a fascinating glimpse into their warrior heritage and intricate hand-tapped tattoo artistry.

4. Bukidnon

In the province of Bukidnon, experience the culture of the Talaandig tribe. Engage in traditional music and dance, learn about their indigenous rituals, and explore their crafts, including traditional musical instruments and intricate beadwork.

By visiting these indigenous communities, travelers can support local livelihoods, learn about ancient customs and traditions, and foster cultural appreciation and understanding. Engaging with indigenous communities offers an opportunity to preserve and celebrate their heritage while gaining a deeper appreciation for the diverse cultural fabric of the Philippines.

Eco-Tourism and Conservation Projects

The Philippines is blessed with an abundance of natural wonders, and there is a growing emphasis on eco-tourism and conservation projects to protect and preserve these precious ecosystems. Here are some notable eco-tourism and conservation initiatives in the Philippines:

1. Tubbataha Reefs Natural Park

Located in the Sulu Sea, Tubbataha Reefs Natural Park is a UNESCO World Heritage Site and a prime example of successful marine conservation. This protected area is home to vibrant coral reefs, diverse marine life, and nesting sites for endangered sea turtles and seabirds.

2. Apo Island Marine Reserve

Apo Island, located near Negros Oriental, is renowned for its thriving marine sanctuary. The community-led conservation efforts have resulted in the recovery of coral reefs and the protection of marine biodiversity. Snorkeling and diving on Apo Island offer a chance to witness the positive impact of sustainable conservation practices.

3. Masungi Georeserve

Situated in the Sierra Madre Mountains, the Masungi Georeserve is a prime example of land conservation and environmental education. It features a network of trails, rope courses, and stunning rock formations. The project aims to preserve the area's unique geological features while promoting environmental awareness.

4. Banaue Rice Terraces

The Banaue Rice Terraces in Ifugao province is not only a breathtaking cultural landscape but also an example of sustainable farming practices. The local communities have implemented traditional rice terrace management techniques passed down through generations, showcasing the harmonious coexistence between humans and nature.

5. Palawan Environmental Enforcement Network

Palawan, known for its pristine natural beauty, has a dedicated network of environmental enforcers working to combat illegal activities such as wildlife trafficking and illegal fishing. Their efforts aim to protect the province's diverse ecosystems and ensure the sustainability of tourism in the region.

These eco-tourism and conservation projects in the Philippines showcase the commitment to preserving the country's natural heritage while promoting responsible and sustainable tourism practices.

OUTDOOR ACTIVITIES

AND ADVENTURE

The Philippines is a haven for outdoor enthusiasts and adventure seekers, offering a wide range of exhilarating activities in its diverse landscapes. From trekking through lush mountains to diving in vibrant coral reefs, the country presents endless opportunities for thrilling experiences in nature. Whether you're seeking adrenaline-pumping adventures like canyoneering and ziplining or prefer more leisurely pursuits like island hopping and surfing, the Philippines has it all. With its abundance of natural wonders, outdoor activities in the Philippines promise unforgettable adventures and the chance to connect with the country's stunning landscapes and diverse ecosystems.

Hiking and Trekking

The Philippines is a paradise for hikers and trekkers, boasting a vast array of breathtaking trails that showcase the country's stunning landscapes and natural wonders. From majestic mountains to dense forests and cascading waterfalls, there are trails to suit all levels of expertise and interests. Here are some notable hiking and trekking destinations in the Philippines:

1. Mount Pulag

Known as the "Playground of the Gods," Mount Pulag in Luzon is the third-highest peak in the country and offers stunning views of the sea of clouds at its summit. Hiking to its peak is a challenging but rewarding experience, especially during the colder months when you can witness a magnificent sunrise.

2. Mount Apo

As the highest peak in the Philippines, Mount Apo in Mindanao attracts adventurers from around the world. This challenging trek takes you through lush forests, mossy slopes and eventually rewards you with panoramic views from the summit.

3. Mount Mayon

Located in Albay province, Mount Mayon is renowned for its perfect cone shape and picturesque beauty. Trekking around its foothills provides mesmerizing views of the volcano and its surrounding landscapes.

4. Taal Volcano

Situated in Batangas, Taal Volcano offers a unique hiking experience as you can hike to its crater lake. The trail takes you through scenic landscapes and offers a close encounter with an active volcano.

5. Mount Batulao

A popular choice for day hikers, Mount Batulao in Batangas offers a relatively easy trek with stunning views of rolling hills and distant mountains.

These are just a few examples of the many hiking and trekking opportunities in the Philippines. Whether you're a seasoned mountaineer or a beginner hiker, the country's diverse landscapes and well-maintained trails provide endless adventures and unforgettable experiences amidst nature's splendor.

Diving and Snorkeling

The Philippines is a haven for diving and snorkeling enthusiasts, with its crystal-clear waters, vibrant coral reefs, and diverse marine life. With over 7,000 islands, the country offers a multitude of world-class dive sites and snorkeling spots. Here are some top destinations for diving and snorkeling in the Philippines:

1. Tubbataha Reefs Natural Park

This UNESCO World Heritage Site is located in the Sulu Sea and is considered one of the best dive sites in the world. Its pristine coral reefs, massive schools of fish, and encounters with large marine species like sharks and turtles make it a dream destination for divers.

2. Apo Reef

Situated off the coast of Mindoro Island, Apo Reef is the second-largest contiguous coral reef system in the world. Its clear waters and diverse marine ecosystem attract both divers and snorkelers. Swim among colorful corals, spot reef sharks, and witness the beauty of a marine sanctuary.

3. Moalboal

Located in Cebu, Moalboal is known for its incredible sardine run. Witness thousands of sardines swirling in unison, along with turtles, reef fish, and occasional sightings of whale sharks. The nearby Pescador Island also offers stunning dive sites with walls, caves, and abundant marine life.

4. Coron

The wreck diving capital of the Philippines, Coron in Palawan, is home to several Japanese World War II shipwrecks. These underwater relics have become artificial reefs, teeming with colorful corals, fish, and other marine creatures, making it a paradise for wreck diving enthusiasts.

5. Anilao

Just a few hours from Manila, Anilao in Batangas offers easy access to beautiful dive sites. Its rich biodiversity, including numerous nudibranch species, colorful corals, and fascinating critters, make it a favorite spot for macro photography.

Whether you're a seasoned diver or a snorkeling enthusiast, the Philippines offers a wealth of underwater wonders to explore. From vibrant coral gardens to thrilling encounters with marine creatures, diving and snorkeling in the Philippines provide unforgettable experiences for nature lovers and underwater adventurers.

Surfing and Watersports

The Philippines is a tropical paradise that offers fantastic opportunities for surfing and various watersports. With its vast coastlines, warm waters, and consistent swells, the country has gained recognition as a premier destination for wave riders and watersport enthusiasts. Here are some top spots for surfing and watersports in the Philippines:

1. Siargao

Known as the surfing capital of the Philippines, Siargao is renowned for its world-class surf breaks, most notably Cloud 9. Surfers from around the globe flock to this island to ride its famous barreling waves. Beginners can also find smaller, gentler waves in spots like Jacking Horse and Quicksilver.

2. La Union

Located in the northern part of Luzon, La Union is another popular surfing destination. The town of San Juan offers consistent waves suitable for all skill levels, making it an ideal place for beginners to learn and intermediate surfers to improve their skills.

3. Baler

Situated on the east coast of Luzon, Baler offers a variety of breaks that cater to both beginners and experienced surfers. Sabang Beach and Cemento Beach are among the popular surf spots in the area.

4. Zambales

The province of Zambales boasts picturesque beaches and surf breaks that attract surfers and watersport enthusiasts. Spots like Crystal Beach and Liw-Liwa offer excellent waves and a laid-back beach atmosphere.

5. Boracay

Aside from its pristine white sandy beaches, Boracay also offers opportunities for kiteboarding and windsurfing. Bulabog Beach, located on the eastern side of the island, is known for its strong winds and perfect conditions for these watersports.

In addition to surfing, other watersports, such as paddleboarding, kayaking, jet skiing, and snorkeling, are popular activities in the Philippines. With its warm waters, stunning coastlines, and a plethora of water activities to choose from, the Philippines is a paradise for those seeking exhilarating adventures on and in the water.

Island Hopping and

Cruises

Island hopping and cruises are an excellent way to explore the beauty and diversity of the Philippines' many islands and coastal areas. With over 7,000 islands to choose from, each offering its own unique charm, island hopping and cruises allow you to discover multiple destinations in one trip while enjoying the breathtaking scenery and pristine beaches. Here are some notable options for island hopping and cruises in the Philippines:

1. El Nido, Palawan

El Nido is renowned for its stunning limestone cliffs, turquoise waters, and hidden lagoons. Island hopping tours take you to picturesque spots such as the Big Lagoon, Small Lagoon, and Secret Beach, where you can swim, snorkel, and soak in the beauty of this tropical paradise.

2. Hundred Islands, Pangasinan

Located in Northern Luzon, the Hundred Islands National Park is a collection of picturesque islets scattered across Lingayen Gulf. Take a boat tour to explore the islands, go snorkeling, and indulge in beach activities like swimming and sunbathing.

3. Coron, Palawan

Known for its crystal-clear waters and World War II shipwrecks, Coron is a popular destination for island hopping and diving. Explore hidden lagoons, snorkel in vibrant coral gardens, and dive into the depths to discover the sunken Japanese warships.

4. Bohol

Island hopping in Bohol offers a mix of natural wonders and cultural attractions. Visit the famous Chocolate Hills, see the adorable tarsiers at the Tarsier Sanctuary, and cruise along the Loboc River while enjoying a sumptuous buffet lunch.

5. Caramoan Islands, Camarines Sur

Situated in Bicol, the Caramoan Islands offer pristine beaches, limestone cliffs, and crystal-clear waters. Island hopping tours take you to breathtaking locations like Matukad Island, Lahos Island, and Sabitang Laya.

Whether you prefer a leisurely cruise or an adventurous island hopping experience, the Philippines offers a wealth of options to suit every traveler's preferences. Explore secluded beaches, swim in turquoise waters, and immerse yourself in the natural wonders of the Philippine archipelago while island hopping or cruising along its stunning coastlines.

Wildlife Encounters

The Philippines is home to a diverse array of wildlife, making it a fascinating destination for wildlife enthusiasts and nature lovers. From endemic species to migratory birds and marine creatures, there are ample opportunities for wildlife encounters throughout the country. Here are some notable wildlife experiences in the Philippines:

1. Tarsiers in Bohol

Bohol is famous for its adorable tarsiers, one of the world's smallest primates. Visit the Tarsier Sanctuary to observe these captivating creatures up close and learn about their conservation.

2. Whale Sharks in Donsol

Donsol, in the province of Sorsogon, is renowned for its gentle giants, the whale sharks. Join a snorkeling or diving excursion to swim alongside these magnificent creatures in their natural habitat.

3. Philippine Eagle in Mindanao

The Philippine Eagle, also known as the monkey-eating eagle, is one of the rarest and most majestic bird species in the world. Head to Mindanao, particularly in the conservation areas of Davao and Bukidnon, for a chance to spot this critically endangered bird.

4. Apo Island Marine Reserve

Located near Dumaguete, Apo Island is a marine sanctuary teeming with vibrant coral reefs and a wide variety of marine species. Snorkel or dive to encounter sea turtles, colorful fish, and other fascinating marine creatures.

5. Olango Island Wildlife Sanctuary

Situated near Cebu, Olango Island is a crucial stopover for migratory birds. Witness the spectacle of thousands of birds flocking to the wetlands during their migration season, making it a paradise for birdwatching enthusiasts.

These are just a few examples of the incredible wildlife encounters available in the Philippines. Whether you're exploring dense rainforests, diving in marine sanctuaries, or venturing to remote islands, the country offers a wealth of opportunities to witness and appreciate its rich biodiversity. Make sure to prioritize ethical and responsible wildlife encounters by supporting conservation efforts and respecting the natural habitats of the animals.

FILIPINO CUISINE AND

LOCAL DELICACIES

Filipino cuisine is a reflection of the country's vibrant history and diverse cultural influences. With a blend of Malay, Spanish, Chinese, and American flavors, Filipino dishes are a delightful fusion of tastes, textures, and aromas. From hearty stews to fresh seafood, tropical fruits, and unique delicacies, the Philippines offers a gastronomic adventure for food lovers. Local favorites include adobo (marinated meat stew), sinigang (sour soup), lechon (roast pig), pancit (noodles), and halo-halo (a refreshing dessert). Discover the rich and flavorful world of Filipino cuisine, where each dish tells a story, and every bite is a celebration of the country's culinary heritage.

Popular Filipino Dishes

Filipino cuisine is known for its rich and diverse flavors, combining influences from various cultures to create a unique and mouthwatering culinary experience. Here are some popular Filipino dishes that showcase the country's vibrant food culture:

1. Adobo

Considered the national dish of the Philippines, adobo is a flavorful stew made with meat (typically pork or chicken) marinated in a combination of soy sauce, vinegar, garlic, and spices. It is then braised until tender, resulting in a savory and tangy dish.

2. Sinigang

Sinigang is a sour soup made with tamarind, tomatoes, and various vegetables. It can be cooked with different types of meat, such as pork, beef, or shrimp, creating a comforting and tangy broth that is often enjoyed with rice.

3. Lechon

Lechon is a festive centerpiece in Filipino celebrations. It is a whole roasted pig, slow-cooked over an open fire, resulting in a crispy skin and tender meat. The succulent flavors make it a beloved dish for special occasions.

4. Pancit

Pancit refers to a variety of noodle dishes in Filipino cuisine. Whether it's pancit canton, pancit bihon, or pancit palabok, these stir-fried noodles are often mixed with vegetables, meat, and seafood, creating a satisfying and flavorful meal.

5. Kare-Kare

Kare-Kare is a traditional Filipino stew made with oxtail, tripe, or beef, cooked in a thick peanut sauce. It is typically served with a side of bagoong (fermented shrimp paste) and accompanied by vegetables such as eggplant, pechay (Chinese cabbage), and string beans.

6. Halo-Halo

A popular Filipino dessert, halo-halo is a delightful mix of various ingredients such as sweetened fruits, beans, jellies, and shaved ice. Topped with evaporated milk and leche flan (caramel custard), it is a refreshing and colorful treat enjoyed year-round.

7. Chicken Adobo

A variation of the classic adobo, chicken adobo is a beloved dish made with chicken simmered in a tangy and savory sauce. It is a staple comfort food in Filipino households, enjoyed with steamed rice.

These are just a few examples of the many delicious dishes found in Filipino cuisine. Whether you're craving savory stews, flavorful noodles, or delectable desserts, exploring the diverse flavors of Filipino cuisine is an essential part of any culinary journey in the Philippines.

Regional Specialties

The Philippines is a country of diverse regions, each with its own unique culinary traditions and regional specialties. From the northern provinces of Luzon to the central islands of Visayas and the southern region of Mindanao, here are some notable regional specialties in the Philippines:

1. Ilocos Region (Luzon)

Known for its bold and savory flavors, the Ilocos region offers delicacies like bagnet (crispy fried pork belly), pinakbet (mixed vegetable stew), and the famous Vigan longganisa (garlic sausage).

2. Bicol Region (Luzon)

The Bicol region is known for its spicy dishes. One iconic dish is the Bicol Express, a fiery pork stew cooked with coconut milk and chili peppers. Another must-try is the laing, a dish made from taro leaves cooked in coconut milk and spices.

3. Negros Occidental (Visayas)

Negros Occidental is renowned for its delectable sweets, especially the famous piaya—a sweet pastry filled with muscovado sugar or ube (purple yam). Other specialties include chicken inasal (grilled chicken) and batchoy (noodle soup with pork and beef).

4. Cebu (Visayas)

Cebu is known for its lechon (roast pig), often considered some of the best in the country. The skin is crispy, while the meat is tender and flavorful. Another popular specialty is the danggit—a dried and salted fish usually served as a breakfast staple.

5. Zamboanga Peninsula (Mindanao)

Zamboanga is famous for its flavorful curacha—a large sea crab often cooked in a savory sauce. Another specialty is the knickerbocker—a colorful dessert made of fruits, jellies, and ice cream, creating a refreshing and delightful treat.

These regional specialties are just a glimpse into the diverse culinary landscape of the Philippines. Exploring the regional flavors allows travelers to experience the rich food culture and discover the unique tastes and ingredients that make each region special. Whether you're a fan of spicy dishes, sweet treats, or hearty stews, the regional specialties in the Philippines are sure to tantalize your taste buds and provide a delicious culinary adventure.

Street Food and Market Treats

One of the highlights of visiting the Philippines is indulging in the vibrant street food and market treats that can be found throughout the country. Filipino street food is a culinary adventure, offering a wide array of flavors, textures, and aromas that tantalize the taste buds. Here are some popular street food and market treats to try in the Philippines:

1. Isaw

Grilled chicken or pork intestines skewered on a stick and cooked over an open flame. It is often marinated in a savory sauce and served with a tangy vinegar dip.

2. Balut

A unique delicacy, balut is a fertilized duck egg that is boiled and eaten as a snack. It is a popular street food item, and while it may seem unusual to some, it offers a rich and creamy flavor.

3. Fishballs

Bite-sized balls made from fish paste, deep-fried until golden brown. They are served on skewers and enjoyed with a sweet and tangy sauce.

4. Halo-Halo

A refreshing and colorful dessert made with crushed ice, sweetened fruits, jellies, beans and topped with evaporated milk. It is a popular treat to beat the heat in the Philippines.

5. Kwek-Kwek

Hard-boiled quail eggs covered in orange batter and deep-fried until crispy. It is often served with a spicy vinegar dip.

6. Turon

A sweet treat made by wrapping slices of ripe banana in a spring roll wrapper, deep-frying until golden, and sprinkling it with brown sugar. It is a delicious combination of crispy and sweet flavors.

These street food and market treats are just a glimpse of the diverse and flavorful options available in the Philippines. Exploring the bustling markets and street food stalls allows visitors to immerse themselves in the local food culture, interact with friendly vendors, and sample a wide range of affordable and tasty treats. Just remember to choose reputable vendors and be mindful of food hygiene practices to ensure a safe and enjoyable street food experience.

Unique Flavors and Ingredients

The Philippines is known for its unique flavors and ingredients that set its cuisine apart from others. With a diverse culinary heritage influenced by various cultures, the country offers a wide range of distinct tastes and ingredients that add depth and character to its dishes. Here are some unique flavors and ingredients that define Filipino cuisine:

1. Calamansi

A small citrus fruit that resembles a lime, calamansi is a key ingredient in many Filipino dishes. It provides a tangy and slightly sweet flavor, often used as a marinade, as a souring agent in soups and stews, or squeezed over grilled meats and seafood.

2. Bagoong

Bagoong is a fermented shrimp paste that adds a salty and umami flavor to Filipino dishes. It is commonly used as a condiment, a base for sauces, and a flavor enhancer in various recipes.

3. Annatto

Annatto, also known as achuete, is a natural food coloring made from the seeds of the achiote tree. It gives a vibrant orange-red color to many Filipino dishes and imparts a subtle earthy flavor.

4. Coconut

Coconut is a staple ingredient in Filipino cooking. From coconut milk to grated coconut, it adds richness and creaminess to many dishes, including curries, stews, and desserts.

5. Pandan

Pandan leaves are used to infuse a distinct fragrant flavor into Filipino desserts and beverages. The leaves are often tied into knots and added to rice, cakes, and other sweet treats.

6. Ube

Ube, or purple yam, is a popular ingredient in Filipino desserts. It has a vibrant purple color and a sweet, earthy flavor. Ube is used in various desserts such as ube halaya (purple yam jam), ube ice cream, and ube-flavored pastries.

These unique flavors and ingredients contribute to the diverse and delicious tapestry of Filipino cuisine. Exploring the culinary landscape of the Philippines allows you to savor the intricate blend of sweet, sour, salty, and savory flavors that make Filipino dishes truly remarkable and memorable.

Cooking Classes and Food Tours

For those who want to delve deeper into the flavors and techniques of Filipino cuisine, participating in cooking classes and food tours in the Philippines is a fantastic way to enhance your culinary experience. These activities provide an opportunity to learn directly from local chefs and experts, discover traditional cooking methods, and explore the vibrant food culture of the country.

Cooking classes in the Philippines offer hands-on experiences where participants can learn to prepare authentic Filipino dishes under the guidance of skilled instructors. From simple street food favorites to complex regional specialties, these classes provide insights into the ingredients, techniques, and cultural significance of Filipino cuisine. You'll have the chance to chop, stir, and taste your way through recipes, gaining valuable culinary skills and knowledge that you can take home with you.

Food tours are another popular option, allowing you to sample a wide variety of Filipino dishes and explore different culinary hotspots. Accompanied by knowledgeable guides, you'll visit local markets, street food stalls, and hidden food gems, trying out a range of flavors and specialties along the way. Food tours also provide insights into the history, traditions, and stories behind the dishes, offering a deeper understanding of Filipino food culture.

These cooking classes and food tours are not only educational but also immersive cultural experiences. You'll have the chance to interact with local food vendors, hear their stories, and gain a deeper appreciation for the diverse flavors and ingredients that make Filipino cuisine unique.

Whether you're a novice cook or a seasoned food enthusiast, participating in cooking classes and food tours in the Philippines is a rewarding and enjoyable way to explore the culinary treasures of the country. It's a chance to learn, taste, and immerse yourself in the vibrant food culture that defines the Philippines.

PRACTICAL

INFORMATION

In order to have a smooth and hassle-free trip to the Philippines, it's important to be armed with practical information. This section of the travel guide provides essential details and tips to help you navigate the country efficiently. From transportation options and communication networks to currency, language, and safety considerations, this practical information serves as a useful resource to ensure you have all the necessary knowledge and resources for a successful trip. Whether you're a first-time visitor or a seasoned traveler, this section will help you make informed decisions and have a memorable experience in the Philippines.

Currency and Money Matters

When traveling to the Philippines, it's important to familiarize yourself with the local currency and money matters to ensure a smooth financial experience. Here's some essential information regarding currency and money in the Philippines:

1. Currency

The official currency of the Philippines is the Philippine Peso (PHP). The peso is divided into 100 centavos, although centavo coins are rarely used.

2. Exchanging Currency

It's advisable to exchange your currency for Philippine Pesos at authorized money changers or banks. Airports, shopping malls, and popular tourist areas usually have currency exchange counters. Be sure to compare rates and look for reputable establishments to get the best rates and avoid scams.

3. ATMs and Credit Cards

ATMs are widely available in major cities and tourist areas. Most ATMs accept international debit and credit cards. Visa and Mastercard are widely accepted in hotels, restaurants, and large establishments. However, it's always good to carry some cash for smaller vendors and remote areas where card acceptance may be limited.

4. Currency Denominations

Philippine banknotes come in denominations of 20, 50, 100, 200, 500, and 1,000 pesos. Coins are available in denominations of 1, 5, and 10 pesos, as well as smaller centavo coins.

5. Tipping

Tipping is a common practice in the Philippines. It's customary to give a 10% to 15% tip in restaurants, bars, and for services like taxis, spa treatments, and tour guides. Some establishments may include a service charge in the bill, so check before tipping.

6. Currency Exchange Rates

Currency exchange rates can fluctuate, so it's recommended to stay updated on the current rates before exchanging your money. Online currency converters and financial apps can help you get an idea of the prevailing rates.

By familiarizing yourself with the currency and money matters in the Philippines, you'll be better prepared to handle your financial transactions and make the most of your trip. Always exercise caution when handling money, keep track of your expenses, and secure your valuables to ensure a worry-free travel experience.

Communication and Internet Access

When traveling to the Philippines, staying connected and having reliable communication options is essential. Here's some information on communication and internet access in the country:

1. Mobile Networks

The Philippines has several major mobile network operators, including Globe Telecom, Smart Communications, and Sun Cellular. These providers offer prepaid and postpaid SIM cards that you can easily purchase at airports, convenience stores, and authorized retailers. Make sure your phone is unlocked to use a local SIM card.

2. Coverage and Signal

Mobile network coverage is generally good in urban areas and popular tourist destinations. However, coverage may vary in remote and mountainous regions. Keep in mind that during severe weather conditions, such as typhoons, signal strength may be affected.

3. Internet Access

The Philippines offers a range of options for internet access. Most hotels, resorts, and cafes provide free Wi-Fi for guests.

Internet cafes are also available in many cities and towns. Additionally, you can purchase a prepaid data plan for your mobile device to have internet access on the go.

4. Messaging and Voice Calling Apps

If you have access to a stable internet connection, using messaging and voice calling apps such as WhatsApp, Viber, or Skype can be a cost-effective way to communicate with friends and family internationally.

5. Emergency Numbers

It's important to be aware of emergency numbers in the Philippines. The nationwide emergency hotline is 911, which connects you to emergency services such as police, fire, and medical assistance.

6. Language

The official languages of the Philippines are Filipino (Tagalog) and English. English is widely spoken, especially in tourist areas, hotels, and restaurants, making it easier to communicate with locals.

It's advisable to check with your mobile service provider regarding international roaming rates and data packages before your trip. Having a reliable means of communication and internet access will ensure that you can stay connected, navigate the country, and seek assistance when needed during your time in the Philippines.

Accommodation Options

When planning your trip to the Philippines, it's important to consider the various accommodation options available to suit your preferences and budget. Here are some popular choices for accommodation in the Philippines:

1. Hotels and Resorts

The country offers a wide range of hotels and resorts, ranging from budget-friendly options to luxury establishments. Major cities, tourist destinations, and beach areas have a variety of accommodations to choose from, providing amenities such as swimming pools, restaurants, and spa facilities.

2. Guesthouses and Bed and Breakfasts

Guesthouses and bed and breakfasts are a great choice for those seeking a more personalized and cozy experience. These accommodations are often family-run and offer a warm and homely atmosphere. They can be found in both urban areas and rural locations, providing a chance to immerse yourself in local culture.

3. Vacation Rentals and Apartments

Vacation rentals and apartments are ideal for travelers who prefer more space and the flexibility of self-catering. Websites and platforms like Airbnb offer a wide selection of properties, ranging from small studios to large villas, giving you the opportunity to live like a local and have a home away from home.

4. Hostels

Hostels are a popular choice among budget travelers and backpackers. They offer dormitory-style accommodations with shared facilities such as bathrooms and common areas. Hostels are a great way to meet fellow travelers and exchange travel tips and stories.

5. Eco-Resorts and Sustainable Accommodations

For those interested in sustainable tourism, the Philippines has eco-resorts and eco-friendly accommodations that prioritize environmental conservation and responsible tourism practices. These options allow you to enjoy your stay while minimizing your impact on the environment.

It's recommended to book your accommodations in advance, especially during peak travel seasons or in popular destinations. Consider factors such as location, amenities, and reviews when choosing your accommodation. With a wide array of options available, you'll be able to find the perfect place to stay and make the most of your trip to the Philippines.

Local Customs and Etiquette

When visiting the Philippines, it's important to be aware of the local customs and etiquette to ensure respectful interactions with the locals and to fully immerse yourself in the culture. Here are some key points to keep in mind:

1. Respect for Elders

Filipinos have a strong emphasis on respect for elders. It's customary to greet older people with a smile and use respectful terms such as "po" and "opo" when addressing them.

2. Politeness and Hospitality

Filipinos are known for their warm hospitality and friendliness. It's common to receive a warm welcome and offers of assistance from locals. Return the kindness by expressing your gratitude and being polite in your interactions.

3. Modesty in Dress

The Philippines is a predominantly conservative country, so it's important to dress modestly, especially when visiting religious sites or rural areas. Avoid wearing revealing clothing and opt for attire that covers the shoulders and knees.

4. Removing Footwear

When entering homes, temples, or certain establishments, it's customary to remove your footwear. Look for cues, such as a pile of shoes near the entrance, to determine if it's appropriate to remove your shoes.

5. Punctuality

Filipinos generally have a relaxed approach to time, but it's still advisable to be punctual for business meetings and formal events. However, for social gatherings, it's acceptable to arrive within a reasonable time frame known as "Filipino time," which may be slightly later than the agreed-upon time.

6. Dining Etiquette

When dining with Filipinos, it's customary to wait for the host or eldest person to start eating before you begin. Use utensils when eating unless it's a traditional hand-to-mouth dish where eating with your hands is acceptable. Finish your entire plate, as leaving food behind may be considered wasteful.

By being aware of these customs and etiquette, you can show respect for Filipino culture and create positive connections with the locals. Remember to always approach interactions with a friendly and open attitude, and don't hesitate to ask questions if you're unsure about certain customs or traditions.

Essential Filipino Phrases

Learning a few essential Filipino phrases can greatly enhance your travel experience in the Philippines and help you connect with the locals. Here are some key phrases to add to your vocabulary:

- ❖ "Magandang araw po" - Good day (polite greeting)
- ❖ "Salamat" - Thank you
- ❖ "Oo" - Yes
- ❖ "Hindi" - No
- ❖ "Paumanhin po" - Excuse me (to get someone's attention)
- ❖ "Pakiulit po" - Please repeat (if you didn't hear or understand something)
- ❖ "Sa'n po ang banyo?" - Where is the bathroom?
- ❖ "Magkano po ito?" - How much is this?
- ❖ "Pwede ba magtanong?" - Can I ask a question?
- ❖ "Gusto ko ng..." - I want/like...
- ❖ "Mabuti naman" - I'm fine/doing well
- ❖ "Saan po ang pinakamalapit na..." - Where is the nearest...
- ❖ "Kumusta po kayo?" - How are you? (polite form)
- ❖ "Kain tayo" - Let's eat
- ❖ "Sige na" - Let's go

These simple phrases can help you in various situations, from greeting locals to asking for directions and ordering food. Filipinos appreciate the effort to learn their language, even if you only know a few phrases. Don't worry about perfect pronunciation; locals will likely appreciate your attempt and will often be willing to assist you.

Additionally, English is widely spoken in the Philippines, especially in tourist areas, so you can usually get by with English. However, making an effort to learn a few Filipino phrases can go a long way in fostering cultural exchange and building connections with the locals.

SUSTAINABLE TRAVEL

IN THE PHILIPPINES

Sustainable travel in the Philippines is becoming increasingly important as travelers and communities recognize the need to protect the country's natural and cultural heritage. Here are some key aspects to consider when practicing sustainable travel in the Philippines:

1. Respect for the Environment

When exploring natural attractions such as beaches, mountains, and forests, it's crucial to leave no trace. Avoid littering, pick up after yourself, and follow designated trails to minimize your impact on the ecosystem. Be mindful of marine life when snorkeling or diving, and avoid touching or damaging coral reefs.

2. Support Local Communities

Engage with local communities and support their livelihoods by staying in locally-owned accommodations, dining at local eateries, and purchasing locally-made products and crafts. This helps to stimulate the local economy and ensures that the benefits of tourism reach the communities directly.

3. Conservation Initiatives

Many conservation projects and initiatives are actively working to preserve the Philippines' biodiversity. Consider participating in volunteer programs or supporting local organizations dedicated to environmental protection and conservation efforts. This can include activities such as tree planting, wildlife monitoring, and beach clean-ups.

4. Responsible Wildlife Encounters

When engaging in wildlife encounters, choose ethical and responsible operators who prioritize the well-being and conservation of the animals. Avoid supporting activities that involve animal exploitation, such as captive animal performances or purchasing products made from endangered species.

5. Responsible Diving and Snorkeling

When engaging in underwater activities, choose dive operators that adhere to responsible diving practices. Respect marine life and underwater habitats, and be cautious not to damage coral reefs. Follow guidelines for responsible interaction with marine creatures, such as maintaining a safe distance and avoiding touching or feeding them.

6. Reduce Plastic Waste

The Philippines, like many countries, faces challenges with plastic waste. Bring a reusable water bottle, shopping bag, and utensils to minimize single-use plastic consumption. Refill stations for water are often available in accommodations or local establishments, and many areas have recycling initiatives in place.

By practicing sustainable travel in the Philippines, you can help protect the country's natural beauty, preserve its cultural heritage, and contribute to the well-being of local communities. Through responsible choices and actions, you can make a positive impact and create a more sustainable and responsible tourism industry in the Philippines.

Conclusion

As we come to the end of this journey through the Updated Philippines Travel Guide, I hope that I have provided you with valuable insights and information to make your visit to the Philippines truly unforgettable. Throughout this guide, I have shared my passion for this beautiful country and its incredible destinations, showcasing the diverse landscapes, vibrant cities, rich cultural heritage, and warm hospitality that await you.

The Philippines is a land of breathtaking beauty and endless adventures. From the stunning beaches and crystal-clear waters to the towering mountains and lush rainforests, the natural wonders here will leave you in awe. The vibrant cities, such as Manila and Cebu, pulsate with energy, offering a mix of modernity and tradition that is unique to Filipino culture.

I have taken you on a journey through the different regions of the Philippines, exploring historical landmarks, vibrant neighborhoods, and hidden gems that are off the beaten path. From the northern wonders of Luzon, with its rice terraces and colonial charm, to the central islands of Visayas, home to idyllic beaches and cultural treasures, and the enchanting southern regions of Mindanao, with its diverse landscapes and indigenous communities, there is something for every traveler's taste.

Throughout this guide, I have emphasized the importance of sustainable travel and responsible tourism. It is crucial that we preserve the natural beauty of the Philippines and support local communities by making conscious choices during our travels. By immersing ourselves in the local culture, respecting the environment, and supporting local businesses, we can have a positive impact on the places we visit.

As you embark on your Philippine adventure, I encourage you to immerse yourself in the local customs, try the mouthwatering delicacies, and embrace the warmth and friendliness of the Filipino people. The memories you create here will last a lifetime.

Thank you for joining me on this journey through the Updated Philippines Travel Guide. I wish you a remarkable experience in the Philippines, filled with unforgettable moments, cultural discoveries, and cherished memories. Safe travels, and may your exploration of the Philippines be nothing short of extraordinary.

Can You Do Me A Favor?

Are you one of the thousands of people who have read my book in the Updated Philippines Travel Guide? If so, I'd love to hear your thoughts! Please take a few moments to drop a review on Amazon and let me know what you think. Your opinion matters, and I'm sure your review will help others decide if this book is right for them. Thank you so much for being a part of this journey.

With sincere gratitude,

Lucas Everhart.

Printed in Great Britain
by Amazon

47879814R00079